Title: Freestyle

Author / Illustrator: Gale Galligan

On-Sale Date: October 18, 2022

Publication Month: October 2022

Format: Paperback / Jacketed Hardcover

ISBN: 978-1-338-04580-2 (PB) / 978-1-338-04581-9 (HC)

Retail Price: $12.99 (PB) / $24.99 (HC)

Ages: 8–12

Grades: 3–7

LOC Number: 2021948450

Length: 272 pages

Trim: 5-1/2 x 8 inches

Classification: Comics & Graphic Novels / General (F),
Social Themes / Adolescence & Coming of Age (F),
Social Themes / Friendship (F)

---------------- *Additional Formats Available* --------------

Ebook ISBN: 978-1-338-04582-6

IMPORTANT NOTE: The illustrations in this advance galley appear in both color and in black-and-white. In the final book, all the illustrations will be in full-color throughout. Some of the illustrations in this galley may be preliminary versions, which will appear in their final form in the finished book.

An Imprint of Scholastic Inc.
557 Broadway, New York, NY 10012
For information, contact us at: tradepublicity@scholastic.com

FREESTYLE

GALE GALLIGAN

WITH COLOR BY K CZAP

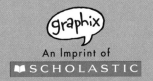

An Imprint of
SCHOLASTIC

Library of Congress Control Number: 2021948450

ISBN 978-1-338-04581-9 (hardcover)
ISBN 978-1-338-04580-2 (paperback)

10 9 8 7 6 5 4 3 2 1   22 23 24 25 26

Printed in the U.S.A.   128
First edition, October 2022

Edited by Cassandra Pelham Fulton
Book design by Shivana Sookdeo and Carina Taylor
Creative Director: Phil Falco
Publisher: David Saylor

For Robin

ONE: THE ROUTINE

TWO: WE'RE MAKING SURE

SHE KEPT LECTURING ME THE WHOLE WAY HOME.

LIKE, COME ON, I'VE BEEN B-BOYING JUST AS LONG AS YOU.

TRUST MY JUDGMENT A **LITTLE.**

SO **WHAT** IF WE HAVEN'T WON ANY COMPETITIONS.

HEY, I THINK IT'D BE COOL IF WE DID.

ring9999

CELL PHONES OFF, SCIENCE BRAINS ON!

ASHA, DON'T TELL ME YOU'RE ON HER SIDE.

I'M ON THE SIDE OF GOOD MOVES.

23

27

THREE: A VERY GOOD STUDENT

iiinhaaale

MORNING.

SNap

sighhh

42

snrrk

AHHH!

bonk

SO WHAT WE'RE GOING TO DO HERE IS FIND OUT THE MEASUREMENT OF THE MISSING ANGLE IN THIS TRIANGLE.

IF ALL THE ANGLES OF A TRIANGLE ARE SUPPOSED TO ADD UP TO 180, THAT MEANS THE ANSWER IS SIMPLE, RIGHT? ALL YOU'D HAVE TO DO --

ARE THEY?

WHAT?

WHY 180?

Exercise 3

25°

x

30°

Find x.

a) 40°
b) 125°
) 100°

THAT'S JUST HOW TRIANGLES WORK.

SAYS WHO?

I...WELL...

THEY JUST... THEY...

66

79

80

86

91

93

WHEWWW.

I ALMOST MISS HOT LUNCH.

THE DRIPPY MEATLOAF...THE FRIES THAT SOMEHOW MANAGE TO BE BOTH UNDERDONE AND OVERCOOKED.

A CULINARY MARVEL.

YOUR GROUNDING TRULY HAS ROBBED US, CORY.

DO YOU THINK THEY'LL LET YOU OFF BEFORE THE HALLOWEEN DANCE?

WOW, I TOTALLY FORGOT. ISN'T THAT NEXT WEEK?

I BET ASHA'S HAD THEIR COSTUME READY FOR MONTHS.

I'VE GOT A REPUTATION TO UPHOLD!

vshh
vshh

FAMILY MEETING.

ching

CORY!

WAIT UP!

SUNNA!

TEN: THE PERFECT SON

WED 11/9

165

ELEVEN: EIGHT BITZ

190

OH, I SAW THAT YOUR TEST SCORES CAME IN.

VERY IMPRESSIVE.

ALMOST AS HIGH AS IMRAN'S, IF I RECALL.

The first time we met was in ~~the~~ science class
And I didn't have a clue
That even though we got on each other's nerves real fast
I'd realize you were super cool

~~X~~ You helped me with ~~the~~ geometry and math
Taught me rock the baby and the trapeze

But none of that's as important as
The fact that we became buddies

I'm sorry I let you down
And I ~~real~~ seriously miss you a lot
I'll totally understand if you don't want me around
And I'm grateful for the time we got.

(I know sonnets are supposed to have two more lines
but these are hard and I ran out of ideas)

Scott Suites

clap

Bonus Comics!

Runs in the family.

One step at a time.

ONE STEP AT A TIME.

Discovery.

You know you love me.

Getting to the Halloween dance.

A very different character journey.

A pivotal moment from the first draft:

...and NOBODY LIKES YOU!!

Gasp!!

YO-YO ATTACK!

ping!

AHH!

You got SUSPENDED?!!

Don't try this at home, friends.

Every day.

me

my husband

it's for REFERENCE

FOR MY JOB

Acknowledgments

Freestyle simply would not exist without the efforts, talent, kindness, patience, and care of many, many people. I don't have nearly enough pages to thank them as fervently as they deserve, so please read the following with as much enthusiasm as you can.

Thank you (*fervently!*) to:

Patrick, for your constant encouragement, praise, treats, and the extra child wrangling so I could sneak in a few more minutes of drawing.

Robin, for existing and bringing us all the joy in the world, and also for taking naps sometimes.

Cassandra, for believing in this book from the beginning, and helping me shape it into something I could really be proud of.

Mom, Dad, and Lori, for a lifetime of inspiration.

Greg, Sonja, Durinn, and Astrid, for always being there.

Mary Alice, for helping me make it to the finish line.

Judy Hansen, for being an incomparable agent and lunch companion.

David Saylor, for taking a chance on me.

Phil Falco, Shivana Sookdeo, and Carina Taylor, for making this book actually *look good*.

K Czap, for using your incredible talents to bring this world into such vibrant, gorgeous color, and for continuing to be a cartooning inspiration.

Taylan Salvati, for incredible publicity work in unprecedented times, but *also* for displaying heroic restraint upon seeing me spew corn bread all over the table during a very professional book tour lunch.

Emily Nguyen, Holland Baker, Catherine Weening, Elizabeth Krych, Faith Sagaille, Erin Berger, Meaghan Finnerty, Matt Poulter, Lizette Serrano, Zakiya Jamal, Emily Heddleson, Danielle Yadao, Sabrina Montenigro, Ellie Berger, Elizabeth Whiting, and the entire wonderful team at Scholastic. Drawing this book might have felt like a lot of work, but getting it *made* and into people's hands is an incredible, magical undertaking that I will be forever astounded by — *thank you*, truly.

Rachel, Ngozi, and Dave, the best lifeline a goof could ask for, long may we quack.

Carey, Ben, Aatmaja, Megan, Mickey, Kecky, and all the wonderful cartoony luminaries I'm privileged to know, for invaluable feedback, good energy, and snack times.

Raina, for taking an absolute goober of a twenty-year-old under your wing and showing them what a life in comics could look like, and for the many years of friendship since.

Mark Kneece, David Allan Duncan, Kit Seaton, and John Lowe, for not laughing me out of the room when I started working on this pitch.

My grad classmates, for the same, may we enjoy Coffee Fox together again soon.

Aurelia, Jordan, Hibah, Riessa, Nashmia, Marianna, and Rita, for decades of laughter, joy, and creativity.

The New York YoYo Club, for a warm welcome.

Neil Cicierega's Mouth albums, with apologies to Robin, who was trapped in the womb while these were on repeat.

And you! Most fervently of all, *you!* Thank you for spending this time with me. It really does mean the world.

CG.

Gale Galligan is the creator of the *New York Times* bestselling Baby-sitters Club graphic novel adaptations of *Dawn and the Impossible Three, Kristy's Big Day, Boy-Crazy Stacey,* and *Logan Likes Mary Anne!* by Ann M. Martin. Gale was featured in *The Claudia Kishi Club,* a documentary now streaming on Netflix. When Gale isn't making comics, they enjoy knitting, reading, and spending time with their family and adorable pet rabbits. They live in Pearl River, New York. Visit them online at galesaur.com.